Best Wishes

William Podmore.

Consall Hall Landscape Garden
The Hidden Valley Revealed

William Podmore

Welcome to the peacefulness of the garden

Relax and enjoy the magic and mystery of nature

Published by
Landmark Publishing Ltd,
Ashbourne Hall, Cokayne Avenue, Ashbourne, Derbyshire DE6 1EJ England
Tel: (01335) 347349 Fax: (01335) 347303 e-mail: landmark@clara.net

ISBN 1 84306 141 4

© William Podmore 2004

This book is dedicated to my dear wife Edna and my father and mother who all loved "Consall"
and worked tirelessly to make a beautiful and happy home.

Print: Gutenberg Press Ltd, Malta

Design: Mark Titterton

Photography: William Podmore

Page 3: Laund Pool from The Folly
Front cover: Laund Pool with Folly and Cottage
Back top left: Azalea Garden showing Bridge and Belvedere
Top right: Laund Pool from the Balcony **Bottom:** Cottage Summer House

A Brief History Of Consall

The Gardens at Consall Hall occupy an exceptional setting due to the extraordinary arrangement of four valleys ranging from 700 feet above sea level at the house, down to 450 feet at the floor of the lowest valley. The arrangement of the valleys forms an interesting and attractive natural site for the house.

The garden planning is still influenced by the glaciers of the Ice Age, as most of the area has a layer of clay from a glacial moraine. The forests, which followed the retreat of the ice, were probably partly cleared by Neolithic man but the first trace of the clearing is in Anglo-Saxon times, when the feudal system of agriculture and land ownership left its mark in the Township of Consall. The markings of the strip system on the ground are still visible in the "Town fields" and the name appears on the estate maps as well as "Laund" which denotes a clearing in the forest.

The earliest mention of Consall is in the Domesday records. The area had been inhabited and the land cultivated, but in the period just before 1086, the land had been laid waste and held by the King. The record in the Domesday Book is, "In Cuneshala there is one carucate of land. Ulfag held it". A carucate of land is as much land as could be tilled by one plough and eight oxen in a year, generally estimated at 120 acres.

In the time of King John the land was held by Sir William de Chetelton and in 1246, he granted the manor to Philip de Dracote; the family held the manor until the last direct male descendant died in 1698. The estate then passed by marriage on two occasions. The daughter of the last Philip Dracote, Frances, married Marmaduke 3rd Baron Langdale, and her granddaughter Mary married Philip, 17th Baron Stourton, who sold the manor in 1808 to John Leigh. He then proceeded to build a new hall on a different site, about half a mile from the old hall.

The Dracote descendants did not live in Consall and the earliest known resident was John Fenton (1517-46), whose grandson "Edward Fenton of Cunsall" was a naval captain under Sir Martin Frobisher; his brother Sir Geoffrey Fenton was secretary to Queen Elizabeth I. The last recorded member of the family to live at Consall was Elijah Fenton (1683-1730), poet and friend of Alexander Pope, with whom he collaborated to translate Homer's Odyssey into English verse. An interesting incident recorded in history concerns the Jacobite revolt of 1745, when the remnants of Bonny Prince Charlie's army fled home from Stone via Consall.

The early development of the land was mostly concerned with interests in agriculture, hunting and forestry. The Consall area was predominately covered with oak wood, a valuable and widely used asset for building and firewood. Later, as the local industries developed, the timber was used for pit props and making charcoal for the smelting of iron. Birch trees were also prominent and the poles used for the local copper refining. The first clearing was near to the site of the present house and the deer park was to the north of the estate. Several of the farm houses were built during Elizabethan times, and some incorporate the head of a man carved in stone and projecting at the corners of the house to ward off the devil.

The Township of Consall had developed at an early date and is shown on old maps before many towns which are now important. This was due

Opposite: Laund Pool from the Balcony.

to the good springs and plentiful stone and timber for building. Later during the industrial development it became very important because of the presence of extensive seams of coal and ironstone and the mining of these has also influenced the garden's development. The records of ironstone mining go back to the 13th century. In addition there was an important source of power at Consall, as due to the narrowness of the valley and the rock formation near Raven Rocks, the river Churnet fell about 30 feet in a short distance. This valuable head of water was first harnessed for grinding corn, but later the power was used in connection with the smelting and refining of the iron ore and for rolling and hammering the iron. Dr. Plot in 1686 mentions in his history of Staffordshire that at Consall both processes took place under one roof.

The Folly from the Laund.

The mining activity fluctuated as the seams were worked out or new seams discovered. The forge ceased working in 1777 when the canal was constructed and part of the original group of mills was buried by the canal construction. In the early 19th century, new mills were developed for the local ceramic industry and used for calcining and grinding flint. However, the mining flourished again when an important seam of ironstone was discovered in 1852 and over 2,000 miners flocked into the area. In 1863, it was recorded that annually between 1855 and 1863, over half a million tons of iron ore were loaded onto the canal narrow boats or sent by rail.

The handling of large quantities of material from the mines caused the trains, of up to 70 mules or donkeys, to be replaced by the early development of tramways, and later railways. One of the first plateways was planned in 1816 to run from Consall to Lane End (Longton) and an elaborate system of mineral lines and inclines connected more than twenty pits in this area of Consall. The plateways enabled a number of trucks with plain wheels to be easily pulled along the track by horses. The wheels were kept on the cast iron plate by a flange. The plates were fastened at each end to stone blocks by metal pegs set in lead.

Later, omega section iron rails nailed onto wooden sleepers replaced the plates, and the wheels were made with a flange to retain the trucks on the rails. The plateway had the advantage that ordinary carts with plain wheels could be driven onto the track and at the end of the plateway could go straight onto the streets and unload at the final destination. A section of each type of track is displayed in the Laund. The mining gradually subsided after the 1870s and nature began to hide some of the industrial scars.

The manor originally had an area of about 4,400 acres. The manor was sold in 1849 to the Hyde-Smiths and again in 1892 to James Henry Meakin. The sale particulars of 1841 advertise 1,800 acres for sale and refer to the many industrial activities and the setting is described in colourful wording: "The nature and features of the Property are part-icularly inviting and its large properties of Grass Land, presenting, from the Undulations of the Surface and the ornamental and dressy Character of the Woods and Plantations, an extensive Park-like Appearance."

There was very little development of the garden when the house was built, as John Leigh had many interests in the mining, the rebuilding of the water mills and the construction of the plateway, which alone cost about £800 per mile. The competition from the canal, opened in 1778, and the threat of the North Staffs Railway through Consall, which eventually opened in July 1849, became too much after Leigh had completed several miles of the track and he was declared bankrupt. John Leigh appears to have struggled financially for the forty years he was seeking his fortune. Had he only survived for another two years until the major rich seam of ironstone was discovered, he would have realised his ambition. Instead a newcomer acquired his assets and became known as Captain "Ironstone" Smith.

The first lake and the old kitchen garden wall were constructed before 1840. The wall was hollow and provided with fire-hearths for heating to protect the espalier fruit trees from frost. Most of the garden planting occurred in the second phase of development between 1892 and 1915. The gardener at the time was a Scotsman and he was responsible for the planting of many rhododendrons and special trees such as the Wellingtonias, weeping ash, copper beech and the blue cedar by the Laund Pool. He also grafted two different shrubs together, such as variegated and plain species of holly and privet.

The gardener left Consall when James Meakin died in 1915 and never returned, until by a strange chance he met with the present owner 50 years later. He was invited back and was able to add to the history of the garden by dating the planting of various trees and the development of the buildings.

During the First World War the manor was split into lots and the farms, houses, woods and mills sold separately.

The Hall was empty from 1915 until William and Alberta Podmore bought it in 1918. They developed and improved the house and gardens up to the time of their deaths in 1958.

Alterations to the House and Informal Gardens

*I*n 1959 the present owner and his late wife unexpectedly had the opportunity to acquire the hall and grounds and started to modernise the property by removing all the external additions to the original Georgian building, revising the internal layout and modernising all the services. The entrance hall was moved from the southwest corner of the building and the two main south facing rooms were made into the principal living rooms to take advantage of the exceptional views on three sides of the house. The original windows had been made small, possibly to reduce the loss of heat, but the owners did not appear to appreciate the views as shrubberies were planted enclosing the house. The area beyond the shrubbery was used for farming, but shooting or fishing appears to have been the major interests.

Even in 1918, one of the main windows closed to avoid the window tax was still built up. The internal shutters had been closed and a single

brick wall built on the inside and plastered to conform to the interior plasterwork. The intervening space was visible from the exterior and was full of cobwebs and dead flies.

In 1959 the Georgian windows were replaced by larger windows, to improve the view of the garden from inside the rooms. These changes meant moving the main entrance from the south to the west face, which in turn resulted in alterations to the drive and the formal gardens surrounding the house. The lower section of the original drive had been made on the steep side of the Sprink Valley and as it was constructed on layers of shale and clay it slowly slid down the slope. The drive was repositioned on the top of the bank directly

Above: The main steps as purchased from a hall in Shropshire.
Left: As re-erected at Consall.
Opposite: The terrace in winter.

(Continued on page 12)

9

Left: The view to the south of the house in 1960. The bank in the foreground was cleared in the 1930s to reveal the original 1840s Laund Pool. The first area of William Sprink on the right has been cleared of thorn scrub.

Above: Taken in 1964, this shows the cutting of the third terrace and a start has been made to open up The Dingle Valley beyond the dam.

Left: This scene records the construction of the new dam to extend Laund Pool. The old dam has been cut through to form an island. Part of the pit-bank has been removed to clear the view to Ladypark but the trees to the left still obscure the major part of the pit-bank.

Opposite page: The view before construction of the Park Folly with the third terrace completed and the pool filled.

opposite the new entrance. An eight room addition on the west of the original building was removed enabling the drive to go direct to the garage to the north of the house instead of going all round the south and east sides of the house.

The site for the rear part of the house had been cut into the sloping land and the adjacent ground was above the floor levels. In order to reduce any dampness in the building, the ground level was lowered and the retaining walls and trees were moved further away from the house. The soil was used to make an embankment to screen the outbuildings and the demolition material was used to build the new roads. The removal of a further four rooms on the east side of the house also contributed to the reorganisation of the garden.

The old garages were away from the house and when the house was reorganised one of the five old kitchens, with its nine flues for a range of ovens, was used as a garage. The original garage, together with the stables, cowsheds and other surplus buildings were converted into facilities for entertaining and became known as the

Halcyon Room. Many interesting and successful money raising events for local worthy causes have been held and the visitors have included many prominent people.

The rest of the range of buildings including the old coach-house, bothy and engine and battery house for the 50volt electricity generating plant were converted into a house for a gardener.

The removal of the drive from the south and east of the house made it possible to bring the formal garden closer and to construct a terrace on the steep slope to the south side of the house, thereby creating a firm base for the building and providing vantage points for the views over the garden.

The view from the house is made interesting by the unique combination of the valleys that produce irregular ridges on each side of the vista. The arrangement is similar to the setting of a gigantic stage, increasing the apparent

(Continued on page 19)

Right: The reverse view on the centre line of the top terrace from the Laund Valley during the clearing. The large beech tree was blown down in the 1987 storm.

Right: The completed clearing and replanting.

Opposite top: The Victorian planting was very close to the east side of the house and completely hid the Laund Valley. The photograph shows the initial clearing.

Opposite bottom: The view today.

Left: The old pool and the house in the 1930s with the old drive up to the original entrance porch. The bank below the house has been partly cleared.

Left: This photograph was taken in 1980 after alterations to the house and construction of the terraces. The level of the water was raised and the bank cleared and re-graded.

Opposite: Another view of the Bridge Pool taken from the Arch Bridge before the addition of the Laund Shelter.

A small area near to the house had originally been levelled and the access drive laid with gravel. The house lacked a firm base and the terraces were planned to overcome this short-coming and to provide easy access to the steep banks.

Opposite: A view showing the terraces leading down to Laund Pool, with early morning lighting and mist in the valleys.

depth of the scene and improving the display of the objects on it. The headlands become the side-screens and the isolated trees on them add to the stage effect and in certain lighting conditions, particularly when mists rise in the valleys, each tree becomes embossed against the background and clearly displayed. The isolation of the trees also enables them to be backlit by the sun at midday or by moonlight. The effects are often most dramatic and beautiful.

The trees in Ladypark form a backcloth with the folly garden as a centre of interest. These trees have been planted in broad swathes of different varieties to give an effect similar to the brush strokes on a painting.

The variation in colour can be most effective in spring when the silver birch produce a purple haze, turning to light green, whilst the fresh beech leaves are a translucent green producing a magnificent effect; unfortunately, it only lasts for a few days before changing to a soft green. The oak trees start as a light brown and gradually darken; the colours of the larch are similar but become more striking in strong sunlight.

In the 1960s many large country houses and their gardens were being demolished and the parts sold at a fraction of the cost of production, which made it possible to obtain contemporary features, such as stone-work, statues and fountains, that soon blended into the scene. The estate was able to take advantage of the opportunities as there were men and equipment to dismantle, transport and re-erect selected items at Consall.

A section of terracing with a balustraded flight of steps was purchased in 1961 from a hall at Ellesmere and re-erected to the south of the house to form the top terrace together with pools and copings for the second or fountain terrace.

The two sentinel trees *Wellingtonia Sequoia Gigantia* at each side of the terrace were planted about 1892.

The third or pool terrace was constructed in 1962 and originally included a swimming pool. The terrace was cut into the bank and as it faced south it made a very well-sheltered enclosure for the pool. A line of arches was built to give access to the pool facilities together with a large covered sitting area, all built under the fountain terrace. The swimming pool did not clash with the rest of the garden and the intense blue of the water did not kill the green colour of the vegetation as it was hidden out of sight from the house and most of the garden. The pool has now been converted to a formal ornamental pool.

The stone façade and doorway on the terrace were originally the front of the cave at Wootton Hall, in North Staffordshire, in which Jean Jacques Rousseau in 1766-67 is reputed to have written parts of his book 'Les Confessions', while exiled from France before the French Revolution. The main staircase from Wootton was also removed and re-erected in the newly repositioned entrance hall at Consall.

The third terrace was also extended to include a lawn with a central sun dial. It leads to several flights of steps down the bank to the lakeside, forming a central axis over the lakes to the far bank of the lateral valley, where in Ladypark an eye catcher has been erected to complete the vista.

(Continued on page 25)

Above: Laund Pool under a layer of ice and mist.

Opposite: A view of Laund Pool to the folly.

Pool Terrace with Rousseau's Cave.

The west end of Pool Terrace.

The extraordinary lighting during a thunderstorm.

A scene during another storm.

A view from the top terrace over William Sprink and The Dingle Valley.
Opposite: A view from the Balcony to Laund Pool.

The Buried Valleys Restored

Once the alterations to the house and the formal gardens had been completed a start was made to clear the views along the valleys and develop the landscape.

The Hall occupies an exceptional site, as it faces south over the main valley with two small valleys joining it, one from each side of the house. This main valley beyond The Dingle joins another lateral valley and effectively forms a compact and secluded bowl shaped landscape, with lakes at the bottom of the valleys, and surrounded by banks with trees on the perimeter.

The garden design has been based on the four main valleys

1 The Sprink Valley on the west of the house, running from the Lodge to the Hall containing the azalea and water gardens and the Arch Bridge with William Sprink on the south edge.
2 The Laund Valley to the east of the house with the memorial and cottage summer house with views looking down to Laund Pool.
3 The Dingle Valley, the main valley south of the house with Laund Pool and Dingle Pool.
4 The Park Valley, the lateral valley running from the Lodge Pool in the west to the Quarry Pool and descending to the Dell. The Ladypark is on the south edge of the area.

The boundary of the garden was extended to include the four valleys, and windbreaks were planted on the top of the banks, thereby accentuating the depth and size of the valleys and at the same time enclosing and sheltering the garden.

Once the boundary began to take shape it was possible to detail the main features and lay out the roads to make the different areas easily accessible.

The garden layout and the landscape were redesigned to reduce the maintenance and to maximise the scenic potential of the site. The garden was integrated with the surrounding woodland and the whole developed with a variety of habitats for the conservation of wildlife.

A landscape garden must slowly evolve if it is truly to integrate with the landscape and it is only complete when it not only provides for flowers and trees but also caters for all forms of wildlife even fungi and the smallest insects and animals.

In the seventeenth century the English landscape garden style started when landowners made the Grand Tour of Europe, especially Italy, and came home to design and build gardens featuring Roman buildings or basing layouts on interpretations of classical literature.

A study of the history of Consall showed that the lives of the people who strove to earn a living from the land and the mines had a major influence on the natural scene. The life of the miners was particularly hard and dangerous. They relied entirely on their own strength, as the only available sources of power at the time could not be used underground and water often became a threat in the early days, as suitable pumps were not available. It is recorded that one day three miners were on the bridge over the river Churnet at Consall and they only had two legs - two men had each lost one leg and the third both legs. Once the materials had been brought to the surface the problems were still great. Handling large quantities of materials reduced the primitive tracks to quagmires and travelling became difficult and dangerous. The pack-horses struggled along often up to their bellies in mud.

The first laws to control the working conditions in the mines were not introduced until 1850 when it also became compulsory for the mining companies to provide education and religious instruction for the miners' children.

The Consall Mining Company erected a building in a field next to the car park, still known as Mission Field, and used it as a school during the week and as a church on Sunday. The last schoolmistress was killed in 1915 when the horse she was driving bolted and her carriage overturned in the hollow between Wetley Rocks and the end of Folly Lane. At this time the estate was being broken up and the building was never used

Opposite: Sunbeams on a misty morning.

again, soon becoming derelict, when it became a readily available source of building materials.

The mining operations at Consall were the responsibility of the Consall Mining Company, generally known as the London Mining Company. Its offices were in London, hence the name London Bridge for the stone built bridge carrying the tramway from the Consall Hall area pits over the railway and canal to the wharf on the east side of the canal. The tramway also delivered the coal or ironstone to a railway siding adjacent to the bridge.

It was inevitable that the people became strongly identified with the area and this has been reflected in the basic landscape design with English features given prominence, any additions such as a bridge or building became a packhorse bridge and a country cottage rather than a Palladian Bridge and a Greek temple. The garden was designed to focus attention on the unique and beautiful layout of the valleys, by arranging vistas along and across the valleys. To do this the valleys had to be cleared, so that the centre lines of the vistas could be determined. The position of the vista was then fixed by selecting the best positions for the viewing and focal points.

The arrangement of the vistas was planned in the same way as a picture on canvas is composed. The eye being led from the foreground interest, through the middle distance, to an eye-catcher or focal point set against a background. The viewpoint in the landscape is often supplemented by further viewing positions at two or three levels. A seat is usually provided to enable the visitor to rest and contemplate the view, and to concentrate the attention; whenever possible the view is framed by trees or architectural features, such as arches or windows. Just as a painting has to be framed and mounted on a plain wall, so with a vista the framing is even more important as the eye tends to wander and is easily distracted by the surrounding scenery. Framing the view from the inside of a building is even more effective by excluding extraneous light, like using the hand in sunshine to shade the eye, and the darker the interior the more the colours appear to be intensified. This effect was first experienced whilst caving, after some time underground in the dark, on emerging to the light and first seeing the landscape framed by the mouth of the cave, the colours were unbelievably brilliant.

In the landscape, colour is normally limited to small areas in the foreground of each vista and this arrangement helps to concentrate the attention on the particular scene. The area of green between the viewing points enables the eye to become refreshed before seeing the next vista and its new arrangement of colours. The distance between views also helps to avoid the distraction of having more than one eye catcher in the picture.

Gradually the valleys were cleared. First the scrub was removed and then after careful selection the larger trees on the centre line were removed if it was impossible to accommodate them in the picture. Fortunately only one special tree was lost, a compromise was usually possible by changing the viewing position or the focal point or as a last resort by pruning. Often a tree affected more than one vista and it entailed many visits to the different viewpoints before making a decision. The same lengthy procedure again took place when later the planting was being planned. The procedure for planting was more difficult and complicated, as allowances had to be made for the eventual growth of the plant. The position of a plant was fixed by a peg, and given a number, followed by a full description of the plant, including height, width, deciduous or evergreen, leaf colour or flower, any special features, and the soil and site conditions. Once the specification for the tree had been fixed, a search was made for any trees which met the requirements.

Eventually the viewpoint was decided and the position for an eye-catcher determined. The design of suitable structures was considered, as each building serves as an eye catcher and a frame; the appropriate use depended on the end of the vista at which the viewer happens to be standing. The relative size of the building was very important and mock-ups were built or the view was photographed and cutouts arranged on an enlargement of the photo. The design and size of the image was then easily varied before selecting the most suitable.

These lengthy procedures were considered worthwhile, as once a tree was planted, it would be many years before any mistakes became apparent, bearing in mind that the life of a tree is usually many times that of the person planting it. Even so, mistakes have been made, and unexpected occurrences have taken place. Two types of poplar were planted to obtain a fast growing shelterbelt but one of them was not very satisfactory for photography due to the pointed top. It had been intended to remove all of them when the inner rows of beech reached a useful size, but grey squirrels have badly damaged the beech and the poplar have been retained. The damage by squirrels has been very serious and disheartening, as they usually seem to wait until the tree is 20 years old before starting to strip the bark and either deforming or killing it. Even more damage and loss has been caused by the human species, but this is not a recent phenomenon, as in past centuries there are many records in the Court Rolls of horses and trees having been stolen from Consall.

Opposite: The east end of the Fountain Terrace with wrought iron gates designed by Alan Knight.

The Sprink Valley

This was the first valley to be cleared. The valley was completely overgrown until the view down the valley was cleared in 1965. The first section was made into an azalea garden on the site of an old pit shaft where the coal had again been removed during the 1926 coal strike.

Following the alteration to the drive, part of the old drive was made into a footpath and an avenue of flowering cherries *"Prunus Sargenti"* was planted. A section of the old drive still had to be prevented from sliding on the shale and a concrete retaining wall was constructed with buttresses running across the valley. These concrete walls at first were very prominent and distracting but they were designed to form small dams creating pools and waterfalls. The concrete was specially mixed to resemble rock and shaped and arranged to represent natural rock outcrops. The construction used over 100 tonnes of concrete and to facilitate the handling, a platform was made level with the new drive. It was designed together with an arch bridge which also acted as a buttress. The platform was supported on three arches so that on completion it could be used as a belvedere with a covered seat in the arches and another seat on the platform to give a higher viewpoint over the valley. A small change in levels makes a surprising difference to the view. The arches framed different views of the garden.

This arrangement of a covered seat and seats at a higher level increases the usefulness of the viewpoint as well as framing the view. The feature enables the view to be enjoyed in bad weather, and has been repeated several times in other places.

The arched bridge was designed to resemble a packhorse bridge and to frame the view. It was built with stone from the quarry on a concrete arch. The arch was built by first erecting a temporary wooden formwork, on which concrete blocks were placed. The blocks were previously cast off-site and made of descending length to produce the curves in plan. Once the last block or keystone was positioned on the formwork, instructions were given for the removal of the support, much to the consternation of the workmen, as the arch looked very insecure. It was in fact very strong and capable of carrying large loads and the method of construction had been used for canal bridges and much earlier buildings.

Originally the stream in this valley flowed continuously, but in recent years the water level in the ground at the source has been lowered and the springs only flow occasionally after heavy rainfalls. The pools were linked together to resemble a small stream even when the flow of water was reduced, whilst the upper part was made in the form of a dried riverbed. The banks were planted with azaleas and flowering trees to form a separate garden.

There were two pools in the lower part of the valley, but the upper one was continually collecting silt from the stream. Due to its position the accumulation was difficult to clear. A new pool was made by the side of the drive, where it was convenient to remove any silt that collected in the pool. The two lower pools were combined by raising the water level of the bottom pool, removing the middle dam and using the silt from the upper pool to form an island.

(Continued on page 38)

Above: A similar view to that opposite showing the effect of framing the view with the Belvedere.

Opposite: The Sprink Valley with azalea and water gardens, the Arch Bridge and Belvedere.

Right: View from the drive of the Sprink Valley before clearing.

Right: The valley part cleared showing old dam.

Right: Old dam removed and water level of the lower lake raised.

Above right: Constructing the bridge arch with pre-cast blocks laid on a temporary frame.

Right: Keystone in position and arch self supporting.

Opposite: Bridge and Belvedere complete and the banks planted.

Above left: A view of Sprink Valley to the west after clearing.

Above right: This shows the concrete retaining walls and buttresses to support the drive, before filling with soil and planting.

Left: The same scene after first planting.

Opposite: The view today. The concrete has weathered well to create an impression of exposed rocks.

The second arch bridge and azalea garden.

A view of the azalea garden from the opposite side of the small bridge.

The Laund Valley

The road from the terraces goes to the east side of the house and continues round the head of the Laund Valley. A number of views have been opened looking down the valley to the lake, each with a different foreground interest and eye-catcher. The verges of the path have been planted so that the views are screened until the correct viewing position is reached. This arrangement increases the surprise and impact of the view, as the scene does not gradually change when walking along the path and only re-appears at the next selected viewing position. It also enables the picture to be more precisely composed for each particular view and the foreground interest and frame made to suit each individual composition.

Two viewpoints have been marked by constructing a memorial with a covered seat and an oak framed and thatched summerhouse built to resemble a small cottage-style building. The latter has a picture window, which overlooks the new lake to the folly. The window casements have been designed to fold back to give an unobstructed view. The framed view from the picture window is much improved when seen from the dark interior of the room, compared with the same view from the outside.

The Memorial

The Memorial is in the memory of Edna Podmore, who, by her devotion and constructive ideas, contributed so much to the recent development of the house and garden. The memorial faces the bank beneath the oak tree where her ashes were scattered amongst the daffodils.

Adjacent to the memorial, sections of the early forms of local rail transport have been re-erected. The section of the plateway dating from 1816 is part of the track which ran from the limekilns at Consall Forge to Weston Coyney and was planned to go to Lane End (Longton). The Tramway was used in 1852 on the adjacent track, which ran from a pit behind the cottage and the embankment, down the present upper track on the east side of the valley to a pit-bank, which filled most of The Dingle beyond the lake. The road continues past the 'handkerchief tree' *Davidia Involucrata* planted in 1965, which flowered for the first time in June 1988.

38

(Continued on page 42)

The view from the Memorial after extending the lake.

Opposite top: The view of the Laund Valley before clearing.

Opposite bottom: After clearing showing the original lake.

The view to the folly framed by the window of the cottage.

Opposite: The Cottage Summer House, opposite the Pool Folly to act as an eye-catcher.

Dell and the Moon Grotto

Nearby is the Moon Dell with a room built into the end of the small cross valley with a moon window looking across the lake to the stone grotto and framing a view of the dell with snowdrops, daffodils and azaleas in the spring.

(Continued on page 46)

The seasonal changes of the
view from the Moon Grotto.

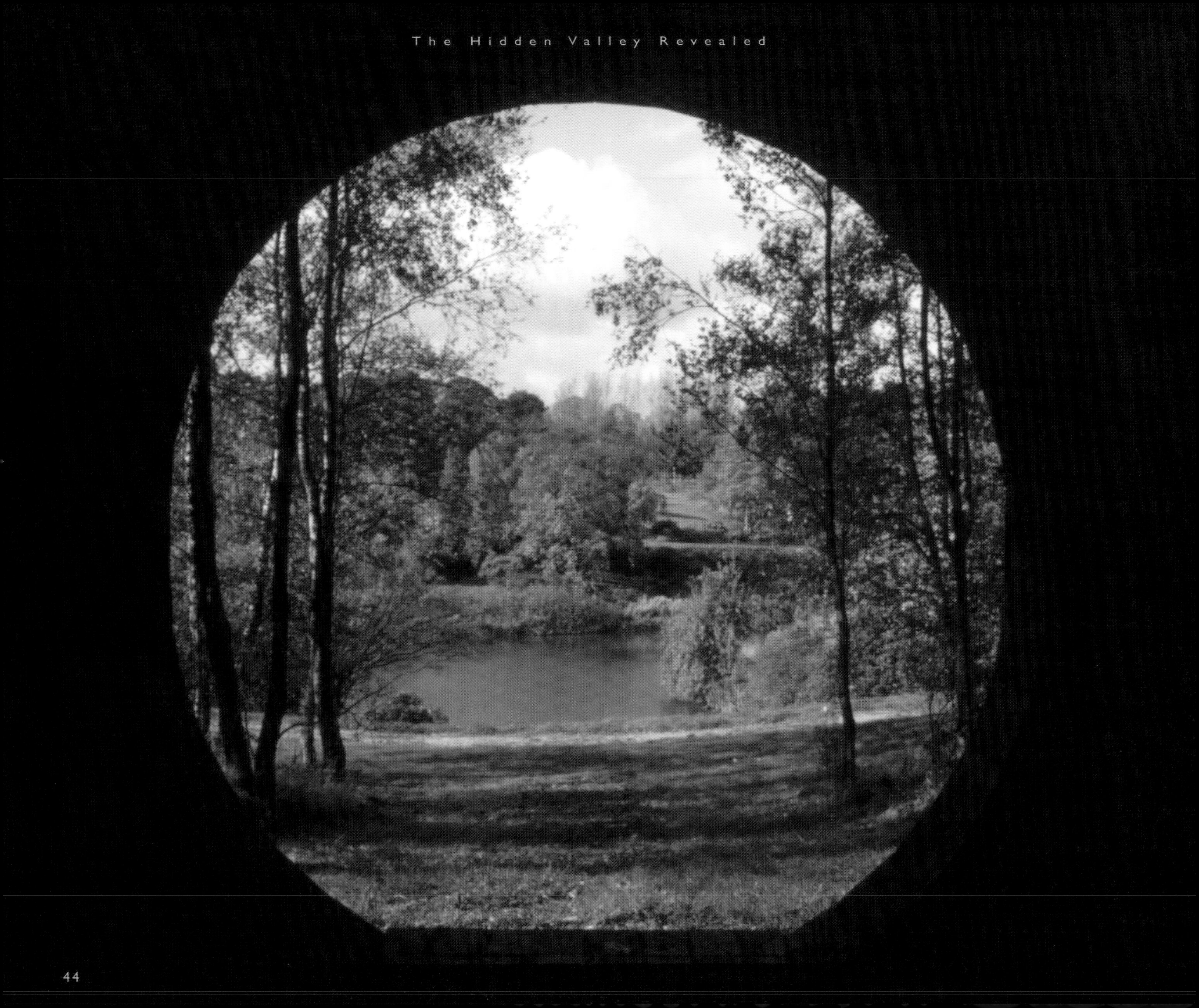

Views from the site of the Laund Shelter contrasting winter and autumn scenes.

Laund Shelter

The steps lead up to the Laund Shelter, built to represent a village market cross. The eight arches frame several views across the lake, including a view up the Sprink Valley with the Arch Bridge to the water garden, a view of the Pool Folly, and a view down the Poplar Avenue leading to an extensive view of the Park Valley and the lakes. A path winds down the bank to the path around the south edge of Laund Pool, and along the south bank to the folly.

(Continued on page 50)

The Laund Valley development was done in two parts. The north section is shown as viewed from the old dam. These photographs show three stages in the clearing and replanting.

The view of the Laund Valley was lengthened to the south when the lake was extended towards the site of the folly, and the old dam partly removed to form an island.

Top left: Taken from the site of the folly, shows the area of The Dingle to be flooded.

Above: Shows the construction of the new dam before removing part of the old dam.

Left: Shows the new lake and island.

The Pool Folly

When the Laund Pool was extended in 1990, the level of the lake was lowered 4½ feet and a new dam was constructed lower down the valley. The alterations to the lake required a new overflow, and to make the circular overflow less obtrusive it was enclosed in a circular tower, with the water entering it below the surface level. A floor was constructed just above the water to increase the safety. The design began to resemble the plan of a castle, when retaining walls were built adjacent to the tower, so this theme was developed to form an attractive foreground interest together with a range of different arches to frame the views over the lake to the cottage summer house. The folly frames were coloured on the near side to add interest and brightness to the foreground throughout the year and on the opposite side a light neutral colour to set off the arches when seen from a distance. This has been achieved by making the arch wall an interior wall and the colouring part of the decoration of two adjacent rooms. At the same time the folly became an attractive eye-catcher when seen from the cottage. A matching tower was added to provide a covered seat and hide for observing the wildlife. The tower provides a seat at a higher level, that enhances the views over the water and The Dingle.

50 (Continued on page 58)

Right: After completing the overflow and flooding. The retaining walls form the sides of the folly.

Below right: The arches of the folly frame the views up the Laund Valley to the cottage.

Opposite top: The site of the new overflow, which became the first tower of the folly.

Opposite bottom: The construction of the overflow and new dam and partial flooding after forming the island from the old dam.

Left: A view from the Blue Cedar to the south over The Dingle to the site of the new dam and folly after preliminary clearing.

Left: The dam construction to Laund Pool and access road to the folly.

Opposite: The work completed and the area planted.

The folly, entrance to the 'castle' with view to the cottage.

Opposite: Inside the folly with the pergola and arches framing the view of the Laund Pool and Valley.

54

The view of the Laund Pool and Valley from the interior of the folly tower.

Opposite: The folly garden rooms, the view in the mist.

The Stone Grotto and Dripping Well

The path from the folly continues round the edge of the pool to The Stone Grotto and Dripping Well. The interior is arranged to frame the view across the lake to the Moon Window. A reclining nymph in marble has been positioned in the entrance of the grotto to add interest to the foreground.

Wishing Well

The path continues past the Wishing Well to the central steps up to the terraces. The wishing well was made in the 1930s. The top is an old bulls-eye window from the oldest part of the Consall water mill. The rest of the well may not be old, but at least the builder must have endowed it with magical properties, judging by the many reports of wishes having been granted!

Many years ago, a young lady came to the house shortly after the gardens had been opened to the public, and asked for permission to show her husband the wishing well. The owner at that time was very curious about the unusual request and discreetly followed them. When they reached the wishing well, the lady turned to her husband and said, "Now George, this is the well where I wished for you to ask me to marry you." Definitely one very satisfied believer in its magic!

(Continued on page 62)

The Wishing Well to Moon Dell.

Opposite: The Nymph in the Grotto Entrance.

58

The view of Laund Pool from near the Wishing Well in the evening autumn light.

The folly seen from across the lake.

The Landscape Garden

The Victorian planting by 1918 had grown and blocked the views from the house reducing the views to less than 40 yards. The screening to the top lake was fortunate as in 1956-58 the area beyond Bridge Pool was requisitioned for opencast mining. The ground was excavated to a depth of up to 180 feet and 35,000 tons of coal removed. The ground was reinstated and replanted.

By 1930 the bank to the south of the house had been cleared to reveal the Laund Pool but The Dingle and beyond were still completely hidden. The area had been heavily mined in the nineteenth century and a pit-bank, 70 feet high, filled part of the valley and at one point crossed the valley, completely blocking the view along it. When the mining finished, trees had been allowed to grow to screen mining activity, but by examination of the area and from knowledge acquired over many years of exploration it was possible to visualise the immense potential for the exceptional setting of the house.

The side valleys were almost cleared by 1965, and work was starting to clear the main valley. As the tree clearing progressed, the unusual system of valleys was partly revealed, but the pit-bank also became very noticeable, and it was obvious that to achieve the site's potential, the bank would have to be removed. In all, four pit-banks had to be removed to clear the valleys. The problem was where to put such a large amount of shale. It was decided to use it to build five new dams, positioned to extend the Laund and Dingle Pools and form three completely new lakes. This plan also enabled any colliery surface working to be hidden under the water.

Right: The open-cast mining in 1957 and after refilling and first replanting.

Opposite: After thirty years growth.

The dams were designed to blend into the natural undulations; the faces of the dams were shaped with small ridges and the top of the dams varied in width and height and the whole curved to disguise the straight clay core which was necessary to seal the dam. Nature does not produce straight lines and they have been carefully avoided during the construction of all new banks, so eventually when covered with vegetation the finished result will not be recognisable as man-made. Straight lines have been used in the formal gardens near to the house, but the further away the less they have been used and then only for avenues. The banks on the sides of the new pools were also altered to accentuate the inlets, and the contours of the banks above the water were shaped to look natural and to conform with the new water levels. The dams did not use all the material and two new ridges had to be built on the side of the valley to complete the clearance. The new ridges up to 40 feet high were also carefully arranged and shaped to blend into the sides of the valley and provide new viewing points.

The view from the Stone Circle after the seventy foot pit-bank had been cleared of scrub and part removed to build the Laund dam. The site of Quarry Pool in the smoke is being cleared.

Islands were built to encourage the waterfowl to nest and to add interest and depth to the views across the lakes. Rock out-crops were built for the birds to perch on as well as facilitating photography from an adjacent hide. All the shale banks were eventually covered with soil, and shrubs and trees were planted to enhance the scenery.

The removal of the pit-banks was a mammoth task, involving the removal of over 250,000 tons of shale. In addition the construction of the dams required the removal of silt and the excavation of clay. Altogether more than another 50,000 tons had to be moved. The work required six machines for over a year in all, moving the materials at up to 200 tons an hour, if the weather was good! New roads had to be constructed so that the large dumpers could transport the huge quantities of materials and these roads quickly became impassable in wet conditions as they were laid on shale and clay. This meant rebuilding the roads several times under very difficult conditions for men and machines.

The foundations for the dam also required excavating to reach a suitable strata. A trench on the centre line of the dam was then cut into the bed and at each end, and this core was packed and puddled with clay to seal the dam to prevent the water in the lake from percolating through the shale of the dam. This work needed great care and attention to detail and it was often difficult to support the sides of the trench and carry out these essential tasks in safety. As the work was in the bottom of the valley, the stream had to be temporarily diverted and again heavy rain produced a host of problems. The shale in the dam was laid in layers and consolidated and at the same time a brick overflow weir was built to collect the flow of water and large concrete pipes were laid to convey the water back down to the stream below the site of the dam. The pipes had to be capable of handling a quantity of more than twice the amount of water flowing during the worst flood in the last one hundred years.

Three of the dams were built on the sites of old collieries and this caused much extra work as the old records of the mines were not reliable and the ground had to be excavated to locate any shafts, tunnels or culverts, and then either fill or remove them. In the case of The Dingle dam, one of several culverts was missed, as at first it was not apparent that the pit-bank had been built on top of two earlier pit-banks, each having a separate set of culverts. When the problem was discovered the dam had to be redesigned and this involved removing a large part of the new dam and rebuilding it.

The removal of the pit-banks not only removed the blots on the landscape, but the water enhanced the scenery and the new roads made the area easily accessible for walking and viewing.

The new roads, wherever convenient, were built on the old tracks and the layout designed so that after completing the removal of the pit-banks, the roads could be used as paths to connect the view points throughout the garden, as well as improving the access through the woods. The roads were built with a lower circuit just above the water level of the lakes and an upper level connecting the higher viewpoints. Trees and shrubs were planted to improve the views from the paths and the wildlife environment.

Above right: Work continues with some of the machines removing the pit-bank to construct Quarry Pool dam, shown partly flooded.

Right: The same view from the Stone Circle on completion. The Dingle Pool covers the bottom of the pit-bank.

The Conservation Area

The landscape garden and conservation area covers an area of 70 acres and lies in a side valley on the west bank of the River Churnet valley and at the foot of the Pennines.

The map on page 78 shows the general arrangement of the different areas and the four miles of tracks. It is difficult to recommend a route to cover the area as so much depends on the seasons, weather and personal preferences.

The area south of the Laund Pool dam consists of four lakes, the banks primarily planted with a variety of trees and shrubs to create a wide range of habitats for birds and animals. An old meadow, last used over 120 years ago, before the use of chemical fertilisers, is being developed not only for flowers but also with specially tended areas for ground feeding and nesting farmland birds which have been displaced by modern farming practices. The three islands have also attracted birds and the numbers and variety continue to increase. The rate at which the wildlife responds to the new habitats is very surprising and makes the work worthwhile. Foxes and in some cases badgers have started to use the new tracks and this makes observation easier.

There are several features in the area including:

The Stone Circle

The Stone Circle was built to encourage visitors to visit the site with a view over The Dingle Pool to the Weaver Hills and the east end of the Park Valley. The viewpoint was rarely found by visitors and, to attract them to the site, a mound was built to improve the view and surplus old stone gateposts were arranged in a circle on the top.

The stone circle has certainly achieved this objective and in addition created a lot of interest, curiosity and fantasy regarding its "ancient" history. Maybe in time, the myths which have been evoked will become a part of local folklore, of past rituals and bizarre happenings! A central flat stone was placed as a seat or, depending on which legend is believed, a sacrificial slab!

A similar view together with a view of Lodge Pool is now obtained from the new Foxearth Ridge. This forty feet high ridge is made of shale from one of the pit-banks. It has been shaped to blend with the natural scenery. On the opposite hillside beyond Dingle Pool is another man made ridge, again to use up the surplus shale left after the dam constructions.

Opposite: The Stone Circle looking across the Laund Valley.

Lodge Pool

Lodge Pool was the site of one of the mines, which in 1850-70 used an early steam engine to pump water from the mineshaft; part of the engine bed was incorporated into the folly walls. The pit-bank was used to build the Lodge Pool dam, and the pool now covers the site of the colliery.

Ladypark

Ladypark is due south of the Hall and The Park Folly consists of a porch from a house near Oundle and incorporates a room with a seat. It is built on the main axis of the view from the Hall as an eye-catcher. The building is situated on a paved area on a raised terrace, with steps on the axis and two stone towers from Ellesmere, one at each end of the terrace wall.

The old stone quarries

The old stone quarries are to the east of Ladypark on a path leading to the east end of Quarry Pool. The quarries were used to supply building stone for the farm buildings and field boundary walls. The large blocks of stone were used for some of the recent development work including the grotto. The path continues to Quarry Pool where there are views from the rock seat on the bank back over the lake to the Foxearth Ridge.

Below: The site of Quarry Pool before building Foxearth Ridge. The foreground has been cleared and a temporary lake formed to control the stream whilst building the main dam. **Below right:** After clearing and flooding, Quarry Pool is viewed from the top of the new ridge. The new access roads have been built on both banks of the lake.

The Dell

Below the dam is The Dell. A series of rock pools is being built in this deep dell, where a range of ferns grow on the rock faces. The Dell appears to many people as a magical and enchanted secret haven, and amongst the sounds of the wind in the trees and water splashing and chattering over the rocks, it is easy to conjure mysterious murmurings amongst the deep shadows and the flickering shafts of sunlight flitting between the branches of the canopy of trees.

Muggets Pool

The dam to this pool was constructed from a pit-bank formed when the shale was excavated from an adit in the bank above the road and adjacent to a group of bell pits higher up the bank.

An adit is a horizontal tunnel driven into the side of a hill to reach the mineral. It was usually at a gentle incline that enabled the excavated materials to be dragged to the exit in boxes; sometimes the boxes had wheels.

The bell pit was only viable when the seam was near to the surface. A shallow shaft was sunk into the seam and then the mineral was excavated round the outside of the shaft; the amount was limited by the insecurity of the material above the seam being worked. The material had to be lifted to the surface in baskets by ropes.

Opposite: The Lodge Pool covering the site of the colliery, and pit-bank.

Kop me Kew

Kop me Kew is the name of an adjacent mine and the bank is a good viewpoint over the Park Valley and pools.

The restoration has been most rewarding and nature once again has been allowed to develop the scenery and each day adds to the exceptional beauty of this peaceful English countryside.

Nature produces many wonderful surprises; unexpected areas of flowers have appeared when areas have been cleared, such as carpets of wild forget-me-nots with stichwort, and patches of knapweed and wild orchids. The changes are often followed by an increased number of insects and butterflies all adding to the balance of nature.

The lakes have changed the scene dramatically, the surface can reflect the adjacent trees and the clouds and the reflections are continually changing. The surface can be stippled by the wind with moving patterns, or change to ice and be covered with snow and the presence of water can promote the formation of mist with surprising effects.

The addition of water has also been very beneficial when composing the pictures. The movement of the eye from foreground to focal point should follow a curving path and the less obstruction the easier the movement. This can be achieved with grass areas or water, the latter has several advantages as once it is in position there is little maintenance cost and water is always changing and producing a variety of effects.

Photographs recording the pictures are very useful because the scenes can change very quickly as nature completes the pictures in surprising ways and the formats are continually evolving and changing. The scenery not only changes due to the seasons and the time of day, but an infinite range of beautiful effects develop due to the sunshine, moonlight, storms, snow or hoar frost. It was due to landscape photography and producing exhibition pictures that my interest in landscape gardening started, as existing scenes were often spoilt because the composition was unsatisfactory; either the shape of the natural scene needed a slight modification or a tree was in the wrong place, or the garden layout was not suitable for picture making. In the early days of black and white photography it was easy to remove or add objects, but colour photography made it almost impossible to modify the prints. The desire to provide ready-made scenes for photography became more than a possibility when Consall Hall became available and the opportunity was readily accepted.

Nature often provides a vast range of finishing touches and the alterations can be sudden and dramatic. It is then essential to act quickly to record any fleeting effects or in normal circumstances choose the right time of day and conditions. The camera is always loaded and ready for action. Snow gives the landscape a new dimension and it also reveals a surprising record of the number of tracks made by the movement of birds and animals.

On one memorable occasion, many photographs were taken from one viewpoint in a matter of twenty minutes as the mist swirled over the valleys rising and falling between the banks and the trees. The different planes of trees were continually changing, some fading and others suddenly appearing. The sunbeams occasionally broke through and acted like spotlights to accentuate various trees or areas of water. Each scene only lasted for a brief moment but every scene was different and incredibly beautiful. An equally dramatic and awe-inspiring change results from the formation of hoarfrost, especially when first caught in the sunlight; unfortunately, once again, the majestic effect only lasts a few minutes.

Opposite: Fountain Terrace transformed by snow.

The photographs bring back the memories, but they can never convey the feeling of mystery and power of nature that such scenes create in the mind. Such memories are ample reward for all the efforts to reveal the natural landscape and enhance its beauty.

Folly in the mist.

The Folly Garden.

The Folly Garden with mist over the lake.

Early morning mist over Laund Pool.

The entrance drive with autumn mist.

Consall Hall Landscape Garden

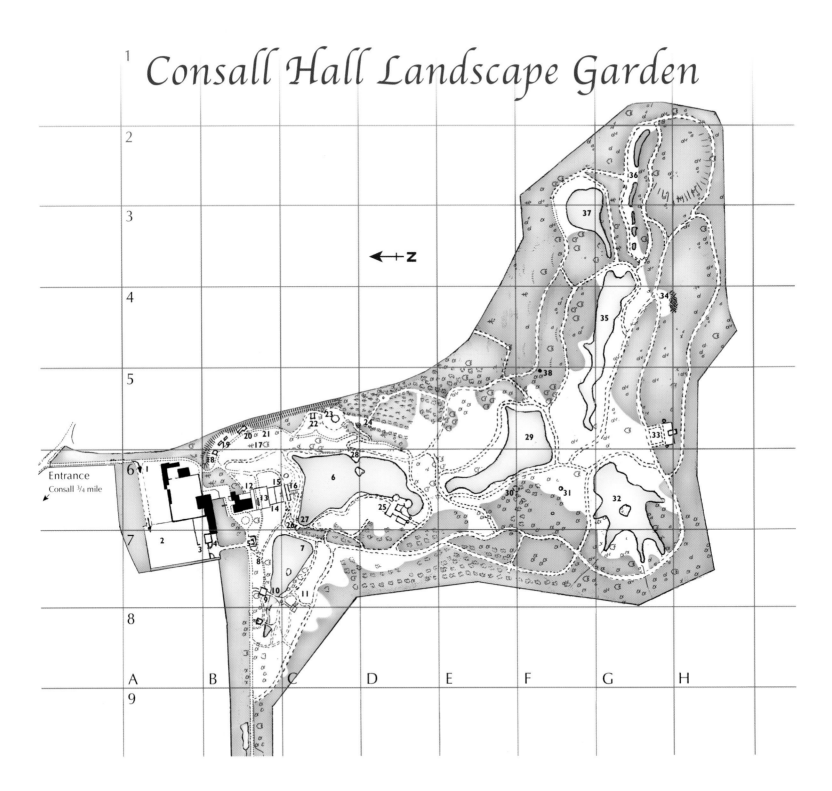

Entrance
Consall ¾ mile

Map Key

Map Ref

1	6.1	A.1	Entrance
2	7.5	A.6	Car Park
3	7.2	B.0	Garden gate
4	7.1	B.1	Halcyon Room and toilets
5	7.1	B.6	Balcony
6	6.5	C.6	Laund Pool

Sprink Valley

7	7.3	C.2	Bridge Pool
8	7.5	B.8	Cherry Avenue
9	7.7	B.8	Belvedere
10	7.8	B.8	Arch Bridge
11	7.8	C.3	William Sprink

Terraces

12	6.6	B.7	Top terrace
13	6.6	B.8	Fountain terrace
14	6.6	B.9	Pool terrace
15	6.6	C.0	Sundial Lawn
16	6.6	C.2	Steps

Laund Valley & The Dingle

17	6.0	B.7	The Laund
18	6.0	B.1	Memorial
19	5.9	B.2	Plateway and Tramway
20	5.7	B.5	Thatched Cottage
21	5.7	B.8	Site of Mine Tramway
22	5.5	C.4	Moon Dell and Grotto
23	5.5	C.7	Laund Shelter

24	5.5	D.3	Poplar Avenue
25	6.7	D.7	The Folly
26	6.9	C.2	Stone Grotto
27	6.8	C.2	Wishing Well
28	6.1	C.9	Blue Cedar

Park Valley (Conservation Area)

29	6.0	F.1	Dingle Pool
30	6.4	F.0	Stone Circle
31	6.4	F.7	Foxearth Ridge
32	6.8	G.3	Lodge Pool
33	5.8	G.9	Lady Park Garden
34	4.2	H.0	Old Quarry
35	4.5	G.1	Quarry Pool
36	3.5	G.5	The Dell
37	3.0	F.9	Muggets Pool
38	5.0	F.3	Kop Me Kew

Each side of the squares represents approximately 110 yards

Gratitude and Acknowledgements

I wish to acknowledge the tremendous assistance of very many friends and workers who
have made the restoration, development and maintenance of the garden a feasible proposition.

It is not possible to mention by name the many hundreds of people who have contributed so much
over a period of nearly fifty years and continue to support and encourage me in the on-going work.

I am very grateful to everyone who has been a part of the team. Even the smallest task well done
is a valuable and essential part of the complete result and is remembered with gratitude.

I am also very grateful to everyone connected with the production of this book, without
whose encouragement, guidance and expertise it would not have been viable.

Visiting the Garden

The garden is only
open by written appointment
for groups of twenty or more visitors.

Apply in writing to:

Consall Hall Estate Office (appointments)
Consall Hall
Wetley Rocks
Stoke-on-Trent
ST9 OAG
England